SERGE NORMANT
METAMORPHOSIS

SERGE NORMANT
METAMORPHOSIS

SERGE NORMANT

FOREWORD BY JULIA ROBERTS

INTRODUCTION BY ISABELLA ROSSELLINI

ART DIRECTION BY RANÉE PALONE FLYNN

HARRY N. ABRAMS INC., PUBLISHERS

In memory of Marina, Denise, Georgette, and Christine.

Half title:
Steven Meisel, Laura Mercier, Frankie Rayder, David Bohls and Serge Normant
Steven Meisel

Frontispiece:
Kate Moss
Sante D'Orazio

Opposite:
Bridget Hall
Ellen von Unwerth

Editor: Christopher Sweet
Editorial Assistant: Sigi Nacson
Designer: Ranée Palone Flynn
Production Manager: Kaija Markoe

Library of Congress Cataloging-in-Publication Data

Normant, Serge.
  Metamorphosis / Serge Normant ; foreword by Julia Roberts ;
introduction by Isabella Rossellini.
    p. cm.
  ISBN 0-8109-4344-1 (hardcover)
 1. Portrait photography. 2. Celebrities--Pictorial works. 3.
Photography of women. 4. Hairstyles in art. I. Title.
  TR681.F3N6723 2004
  779'.24--dc22
                         2003021482

Published in 2004 by Harry N. Abrams, Incorporated, New York.
All rights reserved. No part of the contents of this book may be reproduced without
written permission of the publisher.

Printed and bound in China

10 9 8 7 6 5 4 3

 Harry N. Abrams, Inc.
100 Fifth Avenue
New York, N.Y. 10011
www.abramsbooks.com

Abrams is a subsidiary of

 LA MARTINIÈRE
GROUPE

JULIA ROBERTS
PATRICK DEMARCHELIER

Talent.

A word that applies to so many things, so many people, and to so many different types of work. I have had the good fortune to meet a great number of truly talented people in my life. One of the more amazing talents to me has always been hair and makeup. I am fascinated with the vision, the application, and the ability to transform someone subtly or completely.

This awe comes, in part, from the fact that I do not wear makeup or fix my hair much in real life, and the opportunity to have it done is like a game of fantasy. My hair fantasy, and every girl has one, arrived one day in Louisiana in the form of a sweet-faced French man.

I had worked all night, and, with about three hours of sleep to my name, felt in no shape to be photographed. Taking my place in the hair chair, I explained to this nice man I had known for seven or so minutes how tired I was. He told me to relax and not to worry. Promising the day would be great, he began to brush my hair. When I woke up an hour later, my hair looked lovely and I realized he had taken the care (after I had fallen sound asleep) to work around my slumped head. I felt pretty and refreshed—you can't beat that!—and the day was great, as he had promised.

From one hairstyle to the next, I couldn't believe my hair could do such things! The teenage girl in me who felt her curly hair was a curse and an unfair twist of fate, never wanted the day to end, or at least never wanted this man, who was as dear as he was talented, to leave my side.

That day was twelve years ago. The hair stylist was, of course, Serge Normant. He has impacted my life in so many ways with his fabulous vision and his remarkable skill, and his friendship and tender heart.

Talent. True talent never ceases to amaze me. Serge Normant, my pain au chocolate, never ceases to amaze me and anyone who knows him.

– *Julia Roberts*

foreword

ISABELLA ROSSELLINI
JAMES GIBBS/DICK PAGE

ISABELLA ROSSELLINI: One of your most famous clients—and the woman who graces the cover of your book—is Julia Roberts. How did you meet?

SERGE NORMANT: She was filming in Louisiana, about two years after Pretty Woman had come out, and I was excited and nervous at the same time to meet her—but she made me feel at ease right away. She was tired because she'd been working all night. I was curling her hair and she fell asleep. It was very sweet. I fell under the spell of her charm.

ISABELLA ROSSELLINI: Did she fall asleep because she was exhausted or because she trusted you?

SERGE NORMANT: Well, of course she was exhausted from the night shoot, but I'd like to think that she trusted me too. And, in fact, as I curled her hair and, as I didn't want to wake her up, I couldn't do it in the perfect way, and had to adapt myself to the situation. And in the end, her hair came out in a random curl that I could not have created if she had been standing up. That day my career took a new direction.

introduction

interview:

Isabella
Rossellini
& Serge
Normant

ISABELLA ROSSELLINI: The title of your book is *Metamorphosis*. Why this word to characterize your work represented in the book?

SERGE NORMANT: In ancient myths people were transformed by supernatural power into animals, trees, objects. Metamorphosis encompasses a change of shape, structure, or form. As a hairdresser, I am interested in transforming the appearance or character of someone using their hair as a medium. For me, metamorphosis is all about creating an image. Sometimes balancing hair with clothes or surroundings. Sometimes retreating into the background, making it look like I've done very little. Sometimes trying to keep a real feel, the feeling that you can touch the hair. And sometimes trying to deliver something completely unexpected and crazy.

ISABELLA ROSSELLINI: When and how did you become a hairdresser?

SERGE NORMANT: Oh, when I was very young my little cousins were always around, as was my mom who became my first victim—not always to my father's delight, having done on her, as you can imagine, every hairdo in the book. I loved playing with hair. I didn't really know what to do with it, but I would dream of what I do today—that is, search everyday for glamour. Later, I worked as an apprentice in a salon for three years in the suburbs of Paris.

ISABELLA ROSSELLINI: And how did you get from the suburbs of Paris to where you are today?

SERGE NORMANT: It's strange because I was always extremely shy and introverted as a kid and it's so hard trying to get work at one of the top salons. But, when I was eighteen I showed up at Bruno Pitini's, a famous salon in Paris, dressed in an electric-blue leather jacket and high boots. Really a fashion victim. They asked me to show them what I could do, a question which even today would intimidate me. I showed them what I could do, they liked me, and I began working there. Then I moved from Paris to Pitini's New York salon, and eventually started to do more fashion, working with photographers at shoots, in studios, and at shows.

ISABELLA ROSSELLINI: In the course of your career, were there any slipups along the way?

SERGE NORMANT: Once, early on, I was working with one of my mother's favorite actresses. We had very little time and she was just about to be photographed, and she asked me to touch up her hair. I was completely star-struck and my hand was shaking. So she took the comb out of my hand and did her hair herself. I was shocked, but I realized later that she was simply doing what needed to be done. And from then on I decided I would not be intimidated by any person in my chair, I would treat them as regular people, not as a stars or celebrities.

ISABELLA ROSSELLINI: When modeling, I've always found that the hair and makeup people create the atmosphere for everyone else to relax, and you along with Laura Mercier [the makeup artist] are always smiling and are always a joy.

SERGE NORMANT: It's more than that, a lot of it is about trust as well. If the models trust the team, than they will give a lot more, which will help me do a better job. If they are uneasy or uncomfortable, it will show in their faces. If we all work as a team, and they know I am there to help them, they will relax and have fun and go with the situation. Trust is essential.

ISABELLA ROSSELLINI: I had that experience making Blue Velvet with David Lynch. Some people say that he manipulated me or made me do things that I wasn't aware of and that I did things without my consent. But it was the opposite. I trusted him completely, knowing that if I went too far he would not use it.

Your book is divided into four sections: Portrait, Everything Old Becomes New Again, Life Imitates Art, and Over the Top. Why don't you tell me about the inspiration for these themes and some of the photographs you include.

SERGE NORMANT: When it comes to the Portrait section, I think hair is one of the elements that most defines the subject. A portrait reflects a personal style, attitude, and often a lot about the subject's background.

ISABELLA ROSSELLINI: Isn't that going too far? What about makeup, clothes, and body language?

SERGE NORMANT: Sure, but I look at the hair, that's my focus.

ISABELLA ROSSELLINI: I guess you're right, but hair can symbolize lots of things, it can be quite a statement. Think of the Beatles' long hair, Jimi Hendrix's afro, Marilyn Monroe's platinum blond hair, and Bob Marley's dreadlocks.

SERGE NORMANT: Yes, but I'm not interested in politics, I'm interested in style. I get my inspiration from these people, from other sources too, but I take the elements of a look out of its original context, mixing cultures and periods, and use them for my purposes.

ISABELLA ROSSELLINI: A lot of the portraits seem so natural, like you weren't there.

SERGE NORMANT: That certainly can be the aim. A portrait isn't about leaving the hair-dresser's mark on someone.

ISABELLA ROSSELLINI: Kate Moss is the most naturalistic model. She has that ability to make every photograph look like it's been stolen.

SERGE NORMANT: Yes, in the picture of Kate Moss on the sofa, I had to make her hair look like she'd just gotten up. Bedroom hair. Sometimes the simplest things are the hardest to do. As a rule, I never touch the hair of a model without considering everything else around— clothing, the light, the mood, and especially the photographer's vision.

ISABELLA ROSSELLINI: It's uncomfortable to pose for a portrait, or at least it is for me. It is easier to pretend to be someone else. One of the purest portraits in your book is of Gwyneth Paltrow.

SERGE NORMANT: It's a beautiful picture because of its simplicity. Kevyn started to work on Gwyneth, giving her smoky eyes, so I decided the hair should be completely flat to contrast with the eyes. For me less was more, but I don't have rules, I make the decision in the moment.

ISABELLA ROSSELLINI: Is that what happened with Sharon Stone's hair?

SERGE NORMANT: I cut her hair from long to short. We had worked together for a year, and I was always pulling her hair back from her face, in a bun, a French twist, whatever. I sug-gested she could cut it really short, because her beautiful face could handle it, that there was something in her face that reminded me of Jean Seberg in Godard's Breathless. And so one day, before an award's ceremony, she said, "let's do it." And so we did, completely spontaneously. And a couple of weeks later, history repeated itself—I did the same to Jeanne Moreau's hair.

ISABELLA ROSSELLINI: Do you still cut Sharon Stone's hair?

SERGE NORMANT: Yes, I did for a while, but I couldn't always get to LA, and Sharon actual-ly started cutting her hair herself. Sometimes, she almost did a better job than I could. I think there is a certain charm to a naive hand.

ISABELLA ROSSELLINI: In EVERYTHING OLD BECOMES NEW AGAIN, you have Shalom Harlow play my role in *Blue Velvet*.

SERGE NORMANT: Films, famous actresses, and classic photographs have always been an inspiration. I have often transformed my subjects into icons of the past, which was the theme of my first book Femme Fatale. In fact, you did some of them.

ISABELLA ROSSELLINI: Yes, I did Maria Callas, Betty Page, and Audrey Hepburn.

SERGE NORMANT: One of my most important encounters with old style was when I did Julia Roberts's hair for the night at the Oscars when she won. She wore her vintage Valentino dress. I said, "I know that dress, I've seen it before." I remembered that I'd worked on a couture shoot when the dress was new. That dress on Julia inspired me to create an Audrey Hepburn look with her hair. The thing about these iconic looks is that they are timeless.

ISABELLA ROSSELLINI: It must be difficult getting young models to capture the right emotion in shoots which have references to the 1950s and 1960s.

SERGE NORMANT: Yes, it's very easy for me, having grown up in the 1960s and having all these references from the previous decades and the styles of my mother and her friends. But some of these young models don't have the same references I do. It's a completely new generation, and so they might not even know who Sophia Loren, Farrah Fawcett, or Twiggy are. I always have documentation on the set—books, postcards, magazine clippings—to help them understand the look we are trying to capture.

ISABELLA ROSSELLINI: In LIFE IMITATES ART, are you paying homage to your own artistic influences?

SERGE NORMANT: As a kid, the most accessible art was the movies. I was also very inspired by the paintings of Toulouse Lautrec, Boticelli, and others. Plus, I grew up reading Le Petit Prince and seeing films like Beauty and the Beast, and I've drawn on these sources for inspiration. I think of hair as an abstract art, like sculpture, and treat hair as I would clay.

ISABELLA ROSSELLINI: There is a series of photos of Julianne Moore as the Countess of Castiglione.

SERGE NORMANT: Yes, I've been obsessed with the images of the Comtesse de Castiglione, a famous beauty in Paris in the nineteenth century. Recently, there was an exhibition of the photographs of the Comtesse at the Metropolitan Museum. She was obsessed with documenting and presenting her beauty to posterity. The originals are completely narcissistic, but there is also a pathos. I asked Julianne to play the Comtesse de Castiglione, because she's completely not narcissistic, and that quality allows her to play different characters freely.

ISABELLA ROSSELLINI: In OVER THE TOP you surrender completely to fantasy. It seems like you've put everything that swims in your brain, without fear, without constraints.

SERGE NORMANT: Art should be that way.

ISABELLA ROSSELLINI: Art? Are you saying hairdressing is an art?

SERGE NORMANT: A form of art, yes. I like to think about it that way. And I like to deliver something unexpected on the set. I try to improvise like, you know, a crazy jazz player.

ISABELLA ROSSELLINI: With curlers and a blow dryer?

SERGE NORMANT: Sure, curling irons, hairspray, pins, rollers—these are the tools I use. But, to be able to express yourself, you need to go beyond technique.

ISABELLA ROSSELLINI: The same applies to acting; you learn the lines and you study your character, and once you've done this, you forget it and you improvise.

I've always adored the image of Linda Evangelista as a man and a woman about to kiss each other.

SERGE NORMANT: I've always loved the ambiguity of an androgynous look. On a set, it's always quite interesting to see the transformation from feminine to masculine—physically and emotionally.

ISABELLA ROSSELLINI: How did she manage that?

SERGE NORMANT: She used the makeup artist, Stephane Marais, to play opposite herself.

ISABELLA ROSSELLINI: So much of acting is also reacting. In a film you have actors, but on a photo set I react to the photographer, or I use the hairdresser, the makeup artist, or the stylist to bounce off emotion. If you can't enter into a dialogue with the photographer, you use the people around him, or behind him.

ISABELLA ROSSELLINI: I have one important question: You are bald. Does it have anything to do with your love of hair?

SERGE NORMANT: I am bald. Indeed, I am very bald.

ISABELLA ROSSELLINI: Was it a shock to lose your own hair or was it your inspiration?

SERGE NORMANT: It was not my inspiration, it was my frustration.

ISABELLA ROSSELLINI: Does being bald give you the freedom to concentrate on other people's heads?

SERGE NORMANT: Maybe that's it. Maybe that explains everything.

PORTRAIT

"Some cultures believe a photograph will steal your soul;

this one just might have stolen mine."

— Ellen Barkin

ELLEN BARKIN
LASPATA/DeCARO

KATE HUDSON
PATRICK DEMARCHELIER

JENNIFER ANISTON
MICHAEL THOMPSON

ASHLEY JUDD
PATRICK DEMARCHELIER

NADJA AUERMANN
PETER LINDBERGH

INÈS DE LA FRESSANGE
MICHAEL THOMPSON

ANNETTE BENING
MICHAEL THOMPSON

JESSICA ALBA
MICHAEL THOMPSON

CAMERON DIAZ
PATRICK DEMARCHELIER

FAITH HILL
LASPATA/DeCARO

KATE MOSS
SANTE D'ORAZIO

GISELE BÜNDCHEN
MICHAEL THOMPSON

AMBER VALLETTA
LASPATA/DECARO

CHRISTY TURLINGTON
LASPATA/DeCARO

AMBER VALLETTA
PATRICK DEMARCHELIER

ANGELA LINDVALL
SATOSHI SAIKUSA

SHARON STONE
SANTE D'ORAZIO

ELIZABETH HURLEY
MICHAEL THOMPSON

KATE MOSS
SATOSHI SAIKUSA

GISELE BÜNDCHEN
PATRICK DEMARCHELIER

JULIETTE LEWIS
RENNIO MAIFREDI

LIV TYLER
MICHAEL THOMPSON

LINDA EVANGELISTA
MARK ABRAHAMS

LINDA EVANGELISTA
LASPATA/DECARO

ISABELLA ROSSELLINI
MILES ALDRIDGE

CATHERINE ZETA-JONES
MICHAEL THOMPSON

Susan Sarandon
Fabrizio Ferri

SUSAN SARANDON
SANTE D'ORAZIO

ERSPOON

EVA HERZIGOVA
SATOSHI SAIKUSA

EVERTHING OLD
BECOMES NEW AGAIN

"My secret hope as an actor is that while playing a character my face

will transform and I'll actually become someone else—period.

I never imagined it would be hair that would transform me."

— Julianne Moore

JULIANNE MOORE
LASPATA/DECARO

SHARON STONE
TERRY RICHARDSON

LING
PATRICK DEMARCHELIER

DANIELLE ZINAICH
PATRICK DEMARCHELIER

SHALOM HARLOW
MICHEL COMTE

CARMEN KASS
PATRICK DEMARCHELIER

MEGAN DOUGLAS
RAYMOND MEIER

BERI SMITHERS
WALTER CHIN

KAREN ELSON
VINCENT PETERS

JULIA ROBERTS
HERB RITTS

CARLA BRUNI
WALTER CHIN

CAROLYN MURPHY
MICHAEL THOMPSON

MILLA JOVOVICH
RUVEN AFANADOR

BRIDGET HALL
ELLEN VON UNWERTH

Linda Evangelista
Laspata/DeCaro

LINDA EVANGELISTA
LASPATA/DECARO

CLAUDIA SCHIFFER
LASPATA/DECARO

FAITH HILL
MICHAEL THOMPSON

EVA HERZIGOVA
WALTER CHIN

GEORGINA GRENVILLE
MICHAEL THOMPSON

SHALOM HARLOW
PHILIP LORCA DiCORCIA

ELLEN BARKIN
LASPATA/DeCARO

CAITRIONA, TELMA, ALEXANDRA,
KSENIA, CIARA, JEISA
MICHAEL THOMPSON

GISELE BÜNDCHEN
PATRICK DEMARCHELIER

SHALOM HARLOW
PHILIP LORCA DiCORCIA

ANOUCK, AMANDA MOORE
NICOLAS MOORE

LIFE IMITATES ART

" To work with Serge is both a privilege and a joy.
I would be anyone for him. Anytime."

— *Sarah Jessica Parker*

SARAH JESSICA PARKER
LASPATA/DeCARO

KYLIE BAX, DANIELLE ZINAICH
KARL LAGERFELD

KYLIE BAX
KARL LAGERFELD

KAREN ELSON
KARL LAGERFELD

MARIE BARILLER
LASPATA/DECARO

OLGA
MICHAEL THOMPSON

ELLEN BARKIN
LASPATA/DECARO

LIYA KEBEDE
LASPATA/DECARO

JULIANNE MOORE
LASPATA/DECARO

JULIANNE MOORE
LASPATA/DECARO

SHALOM HARLOW
PHILIP LORCA DiCORCIA

CECILE CASSEL
MICHAEL THOMPSON

MAGGIE RIZER
PATRICK DEMARCHELIER

LIISA WINKLER
PATRICK DEMARCHELIER

KAREN ELSON
PATRICK DEMARCHELIER

MARIA CARLA
PATRICK DEMARCHELIER

ERIN O'CONNOR
PATRICK DEMARCHELIER

FRIDA
PATRICK DEMARCHELIER

BRIDGET HALL
PATRICK DEMARCHELIER

CHANDRA NORTH
JAMES HOUSTON

OVER THE TOP

"I feel like the queen of a very small country,
and all of the people live in my hair."

— *Julia Roberts*

JADE PARFITT
DAVID ARMSTRONG

CHANDRA NORTH
JAMES HOUSTON

LIDA EGOROVA
RUVEN AFANADOR

LIDA EGOROVA
RUVEN AFANADOR

EVA RICCOBONO
PATRICK DEMARCHELIER

ANNE V
PATRICK DEMARCHELIER

HELENA CHRISTENSEN
LASPATA/DECARO

KIRSTY HUME
JAMES MOORE

LINDA EVANGELISTA
LASPATA/DECARO

GUINEVERE VAN SEENUS
MICHEAL THOMPSON

RIE RASMUSSEN
MICHAEL THOMPSON

CAROLINE RIBEIRO
PATRICK DEMARCHELIER

KIRSTEN OWEN
SATOSHI SAIKUSA

KIM LEMANTON
DAH LEN

STELLA TENNANT
MICHAEL THOMPSON

HANNELORE
MICHAEL THOMPSON

LIYA KEBEDE
NICOLAS MOORE

ISABELLA ROSSELLINI
ERIC BOWMAN

KAROLINA KURKOVA
MICHAEL THOMPSON

comment

While a regular hairdo is good to wear for a month, week, night—a modern hair sculpture lasts only a moment, captured forever with a camera. The hair is, of all human parts, the most susceptible to transformation if there is plenty of it. Hair sculptures can be quite heavy and elaborate monstrosities that sweep you off your flimsy high heels. At best, they are a genuine or symbolic expression of a character or mood. Hair sculpting seems to be an ancient craft. Many a fashion shoot today is inspired by the court of Tutankhamun or the concubines of the Tokugawa Shoguns. Roman matrons, Baroque ladies, the Pompadour, and even gents like Mozart wore pompously decorated wigs of the kind that give you seizures in the summer. In a male-dominated world of artificiality and beauty worship, her masks and wigs, veils and laces, looks and deceptions were a woman's only power tools. Wigged ladies in tight corsets used to faint all the way up to the nineteenth century, a period called the Industrial Revolution, when it became the fashion to show off with a car instead of a wig. The business of sculpting hair retreated into its native domains: Opera and Theater. But it also quickly conquered the new evolving mass media of photography and film. We all adored Marlene Dietrich, Greta Garbo, and Joan Crawford—crowned by immaculate hair aureoles—in the Church of Flickering Light, before realism made a comeback and the era of glamour in movies ended. We must not forget to mention my friend John Waters and his no budget trash-classic movie Hairspray, and do justice to the genre. But sex sells and hair is sexy. The contemporary realm for imperial fantasy and sexual courtship in the mass media is thus always in the fashion world. Fashion is artificiality and deception that exploit beauty worship. She is the perfect union of the sibling arts that decorate and, at times, transform women. Therefore the few distinguished hair sculptors are celebrities in her Pantheon like many models, designers, and photographers.

-Veruschka

Metamorphosis happens on a photo shoot, whether it's a simple portrait or an extravagant fashion spread. Metamorphosis happens when a team of hairdressers, make up artists, stylists, model, and photographer all get excited and put their efforts and skills into creating that singular image, that one moment that makes a great picture.

To be allowed on a shoot to transform someone into an exotic fantasy (as ephemeral as it is) is a wonderful experience. I'm so grateful to have had the chance to work with so many talented people as they've helped me get better at what I do.

Throughout the years, my work has been influenced by many images—from an old master painting to fashion spreads from the 1960s and 70s—and many hairdressers, like Kenneth, Alexander of Paris, The Carita Sisters, Ara Gallant, and Vidal Sassoon, to name only a few. One hairdresser in particular had a strong impact on my life, Bruno Pittini, my mentor. I remember a saying from his school that still follows me today, "Learn the technique, digest it, then forget it"—that is the way to make it your own. Individualism has always been my priority; I love looking at the past and the present to create the look of tomorrow.

I'm lucky to be realizing a childhood dream and making a living at it. I feel blessed to have worked with so many beautiful women throughout the years, and I would not have been able to sculpt their hair without their open minds, trust, and love.

– Serge Normant

ACKNOWLEDGEMENTS

First, I would like to thank all the beautiful actresses and models who appear in this book. I am deeply touched by their participation.

I would like to thank in particular Julia Roberts for her support and friendship, and for being such an inspiration; Isabella Rossellini for being there throughout this project and for making each shoot so beautiful; Veruschka for her trust and beauty; Sarah Jessica Parker for her beauty and friendship; Ellen Barkin and Julianne Moore for making every woman more beautiful than the last, and for being good friends.

Thanks to all the photographers who participated in this book. I'm forever grateful to Michael Thompson for his trust, generosity, and friendship over the years, and for helping me to be who I am today; to Patrick Demarchelier for his generosity; to Karl Lagerfeld for making each shoot a learning experience, and to his staff, Eric Pfunder and Isabelle Ries.

Special thanks to Ranée Flynn for her support, talent, and guidance throughout this project; to Laura Mercier for reminding me what beauty is all about, and, most of all, for her unconditional love; to Christopher Sweet from Harry N. Abrams, without whom this project would not be, and for his friendship and talent; also at Harry N. Abrams, to Sigi Nacson and Jutta Pakenis; to Marie Barriler for her always inspiring beauty and affection; to Damiano Biella for his talent and amazing eye; to Marcy Engelman for always helping me make the right choice; to Flair magazine, especially Alex Gonzales Raoul Martinez for giving me the opportunity to go further; to Monica Delfini for her talent and brush; to Danielle Dennihy for all her precious help on this book; to Kelly O'Bosky Hass, Jed Root, and Jean Francois Raffali.

Thanks to Rocco Laspata and Charles DeCaro for their talent, friendship, and for making this book more special by their participation; to all their staff, D.P. David Dougan, Tara Rooser, Anne Erickson, Denise Gallagher, Mark Engels, and Heidi Parker; to Steve Pandolri and his staff at Digital Color Concepts for their creative skill in scanning, retouching, and image manipulation; to Drive In Studio, Milk Studio, Splashlight Studio, Broderson Backdrops, Mark Markheim (for their black and white film developing and printing); to LTI (color film developing and printing), and Ben Bettenhausen at Print 2 Print.

A special thanks to Paul Cavaco and Linda Wells for their trust and support.

I am grateful to Karen Lesage for making such beautiful clothes for this project; to Simon de Beaupres for his support and friendship; to Paco Rabanne for letting me use his one-of-a-kind outfit.

Special thanks to all the following people for their help one way or another on this book. First to my family, George, Marc, Valerie, and Jeanine Normant, my godsons Robin and Axel Kahyat, my goddaughter Victoria Feli; to my friends Michele Guignard, Daniele Rouillè, Jacky Michot, Danielle Lefranc, Steve and Patty Aviano; to Eric, Anne-Brigitte, and Penelope Feli; to Genevieve Herr, Kevin O'Brien, Jacques and Liliane Pontac, Barbara Baumel, Delphine Treanton, Freidi Le ba, Sandy Lynter, Maria Bartiromo, Lauren Plotkin, Bruce and Sophie Nadell, Sheryl Bailey, Brigitte Reiss-Anderson, Mildred and Angelo Dicaro, Carlyne Cerf de Duzzel, Marina Schiano, Tiziana Trischitta, Larissa Trischitta, Christine Morchand, Silvia Sini, Kenneth Harris, Pascal Daugin and his staff, Jennifer Steffancin, Dennis Freedman, Joe Zee, Tim Priano, Dick Page, Erik Asla, Amrita Chavda, Tonne Goodman, Gerard Santos, Tom Bell, Eric at Herb Ritts, and Denise Markey.

Thanks to the model agencies: IMG, Next, Elite, Marilyn Gaultier, Woman, Karin's, Metropolitan, Pauline's, Wilhelmina, DNA, One Model Management, Company Management, and Lisa Jacobson at UTA; to the publicists: Steven Huvane, Brad Cafarelli Pat Kingsley, Sam Cohn, Nanci Ryder, Sandra Westerman, Nicole King, Karin Smith, Cece Yorke, Annette Wolfe, Carri Ross, Andrea Nelson, Cindy Berger, Lisa Kasteler, Nancy Lannios, Nancy Seltzer, and Ina Treciokas; and to the designers: Alexander McQueen, Betsey Johnson, Calvin Klein, Celine, Chanel, Christian Dior, Christian Lacroix, Dolce & Gabbana, Donna Karan, Gianfranco Ferré, Giorgio Armani, Gucci, Halston, Karl Largerfeld, Louis Feraud, Michael Kors, Norma Kamali, Ralph Lauren, Sonia Rykiel, Thierry Mugler, Yves Saint Laurent, Valentino, XOXO, and Paco Rabanne.

Thanks to the magazines: W, Vogue, British Vogue, German Vogue, French Vogue, Italian Vogue, French Elle, British Elle, Allure, Jane, Harper's Bazaar, Glamour, Italian Glamour, Marie Claire, Flair, Citizen K, Numero, Vanity Fair, In Style, Arena, Interview, Rolling Stone, and Premiere.

CREDITS:

Laura Mercier, makeup / Charles DeCaro, stylist:
pp. 58–59, 84–85, 98–99, 111, 113, 152–153
Dick Page, makeup / Vanessa Moore, stylist: p. 8
Linda Hay, makeup / Andrew Richardson, stylist:
pp. 2, 30–31
Laura Mercier, makeup / Brana Wolf, stylist: p. 1
Denise Markey, makeup / Charles DeCaro, stylist:
pp. 16–17, 82, 88, 96–97, 120–121, 126–127, 165
Diane Kendal, makeup / Michel Bolbol, stylist: pp. 18–19
Diane Kendal, makeup / Alex White, stylist: p. 43
Kevyn Aucoin, makeup / Tonne Goodman, stylist: p. 6
Kevyn Aucoin, makeup / Kilhe Brewster, stylist: p. 39
Gucci Westman, makeup / Michel Bolbol, stylist: p. 28
Diane Kendal, makeup / Paul Cavaco, stylist: p. 25
Virginia Young, makeup / Jo Zee, stylist: pp. 32,
136–137, 138–139
Laura Mercier, makeup: pp. 26–27
Fulvia Farrolfi, makeup / Fredi Leiba, stylist: pp. 54–55
Charles DeCaro, stylist: p. 49
Jacques Clement, makeup / Marie Amelie Sauvé,
Stylist p. 23
Stephane Marais, makeup: p. 22
Thierry Mauduit, makeup / Jenny Capitain, stylist: p. 41
Paul Starr, makeup / Sara Jane Hoare, stylist: p. 56
Brigitte Reiss-Anderson, makeup / Charles DeCaro, stylist:
pp. 29, 63, 129, 130–131, 133
Scott Andrew, makeup / Jo Zee, stylist: p. 24
Scott Andrew, makeup / Alexandra Loyd, stylist: p. 46
Laura Mercier, makeup / Lisa Von Weis, stylist: p. 40
Charles DeCaro, stylist: p. 34
Michel Bolbol, stylist: p. 57
Charles DeCaro, stylist: p. 35
Laura Mercier, makeup / Robertino Trovati, stylist: p. 55
Dick Page, makeup / Paul Cavaco, stylist: pp. 33, 37
Laura Mercier, makeup / Paul Cavaco, stylist: pp. 47, 52–53
Virginia Young, makeup / Katie Mossman, stylist:
pp. 45, 102–103
Brigitte Reiss-Anderson, makeup / Tonne Goodman,
stylist: p. 36
Scott Andrew, makeup / Bill Mullen, stylist: p. 20
Diane Kendal, makeup / Elisa Santisi, stylist: p. 38
Fulvia Farolfi, makeup / Sara Jane Hoare, stylist: pp. 42,
66–67, 114–117

Kevin Aucoin, makeup / Michel Bolbol, stylist: p. 21
Dick Page, makeup / Monica Pillosio, stylist: p. 78
Dick Page, makeup / Michel Bolbol, stylist: pp. 94–95,
104–105, 134–135
François Nars, makeup / Marina Schiano, stylist: p. 76
Kevin Aucoin, makeup / Brana Wolf, stylist: pp. 64–65
Anna Dello Russo, stylist: pp. 69, 77, 87
Dick Page, makeup / Monica Delfini, stylist: pp. 90–91,
100–101, 160–161, 171
Stephane Marais, makeup / Charles DeCaro, stylist:
pp. 83, 169
Virginia Young, makeup / Paul Cavaco, stylist:
pp. 86, 92–93
Lucia Pieroni, makeup / Alice Gentilucci, stylist: pp. 5, 80–81
James Kiliardos, makeup / Polly Mellen, stylist: p. 73
Jeannia Robinette, makeup / Monica Delfini, stylist: p. 176
Susan Giordano, makeup / Sara Jane Hoare,
stylist: pp. 70–71
Dick Page, makeup / Charles DeCaro, stylist: pp. 89, 18–19
Diane Kendal, makeup / Marcus Von Ackerman,
stylist: pp. 118–119
Sharon Dowsett, makeup / Tonne Goodman, stylist: p. 123
James Kaliandos, makeup: pp. 142–143, 145, 147
Christian McCulloch, makeup: pp. 144, 146
Christian McCulloch, makeup / Jill Davidson, stylist: p. 141
Stephane Marais, makeup / Delphine Treanton,
stylist: pp. 124–125
Dick Page, makeup: pp. 170, 180–181
Virginia Young, makeup / Vanessa Moore, stylist: p. 154
Fulvia Farolfi, makeup / Tiina Laakkonen, stylist: p. 155
Charlotte Willer, makeup / Caroline Van Der Voot, stylist:
pp. 156–159
Stephane Marais, makeup / Franck Benhamou, stylist:
pp. 162–163
Val Garland, makeup / Joe Zee, stylist: pp. 166–167
Romy Soleimani, makeup / Paul Cavaco, stylist:
pp. 106–107, 178–179
Brigitte Reiss-Anderson, makeup / Katie Mossman,
stylist: p. 172
Maria Olsson, makeup / Kate Phelan, stylist: pp. 74–75
Kay Montano, makeup / Michel Bolbol, stylist: p. 173
Scott Andrew, makeup / Monica Delfini, stylist:
pp. 182–183, 192
Laura Mercier, makeup / Cathy Dixon, stylist: pp. 174–175
Virginia Young, makeup / Monica Pillosio, stylist: p. 177

Caravan, earrings: pp. 58–59

Laura Mercier, makeup / Badgley Mischka, gown / José and Maria Barrera, tiara: p. 153

Laura Mercier, makeup / Karen LeSage, dress: pp. 111, 113

Denise Markey, makeup / J. Mendel, fox stole: pp. 96–97

Denise Markey, makeup / Anne Fontaine, shirt: pp. 16–17

Denise Markey, makeup / Paco Rabanne, clothing: p. 165

Denise Markey, makeup / Valentino, lace skirt / Vivien Westwood, corset and crinoline / José and Maria Barrera, all accessories: pp. 120–121

Brigitte Reiss-Anderson, makeup / Fred Leighton, jewelry: p. 129

Brigitte Reiss-Anderson, makeup / Emanuel Ungaro, blouse / Fred Leighton, brooch / José and Maria Barrera, necklace and earrings; p. 63

Brigitte Reiss-Anderson, makeup / Karen LeSage, cape and skirt / Stephen Dweck, ring / José and Maria Barrera, crown, necklace, earrings, fan; p. 133

Brigitte Reiss-Anderson, makeup / Adrienne Landau, cape / Stephen Dweck, ring / José and Maria Barrera, feather brooch; pp. 130–131

Dick Page, makeup / La Petite Coquette, corset: pp. 184–185

KAROLINA KURKOVA
MICHAEL THOMPSON